ill lit

Other books and chapbooks by Franz Wright

Poems

Tapping the White Cane of Solitude
The Earth Without You
8 Poems
The One Whose Eyes Open When You Close Your Eyes
Going North in Winter
Entry in an Unknown Hand
And Still the Hand Will Sleep in its Glass Ship
The Night World & the Word Night
Rorschach Test
Knell

Translations

Jarmilla. Flies: 10 Prose Poems by Erica Pedretti
The Life of Mary (poems by Rainer Maria Rilke)
The Unknown Rilke
No Siege Is Absolute (poems by Rene Char)

ill lit

Selected & New Poems

FRANZ WRIGHT

OBERLIN COLLEGE PRESS

http://www.oberlin.edu/~ocpress

Publication of this book was supported by grants from the Eric Mathieu
King Fund of The Academy of American Poets, and from the Ohio Arts
Council.

Ohio Arts Council
A STATE AGENCY
THAT SUPPORTS PUBLIC
PROGRAMS IN THE ARTS

Library of Congress Cataloging-in-Publication Data

Wright, Franz
       Ill Lit: Selected and New Poems/Franz Wright.
       (The FIELD Poetry Series v. 7)
       I. Title. II. Series.

LC: 98-87893
ISBN: Cloth: 0-932440-82-7
          Paper: 0-932440-83-5

CONTENTS

from *The Night World and the Word Night* (1993)

from *Rorschach Test* (1995)

Translations

New Poems

One must never desire suffering. No, you have only to remain in the condition of praying for happiness on earth. If a man desire suffering, then it is as though he were able by himself to solve this terror: —that suffering is the characteristic of God's love. And that is precisely what he cannot do . . .

Kierkegaard

from

The One Whose Eyes Open
When You Close Your Eyes (1982)

ASKING FOR MY YOUNGER BROTHER

I never did find you.
I later heard how you'd wandered the streets
for weeks, washing dishes before you got fired;
taking occasional meals at the Salvation Army
with the other diagnosed. How on one particular night
you won four hundred dollars at cards:
how some men followed you and beat you up,
leaving you unconscious in an alley
where you were wakened by police
and arrested for vagrancy, for being tired
of getting beaten up at home.
I'd dreamed you were dead,
and started to cry.
I couldn't exactly phone Dad.
I bought a pint of bourbon
and asked for you all afternoon in a blizzard.
In hell
Dante had words with the dead,
although
they had no bodies
and he could not touch them, nor they him.
A man behind the ticket counter
in the Greyhound terminal
pointed to one of the empty seats, where
someone who looked like me sometimes sat down
among the people waiting to depart.
I don't know why I write this.
With it comes the irrepressible desire
to write nothing, to remember nothing;
there is even the desire
to walk out in some field and bury it
along with all my other so-called
poems, which help no one—
where each word will blur
into earth finally,
where the mind that voiced them
and the hand that took them down will.
So what. I left
the bus fare back
to Sacramento with this man,
and asked him
to give it to you.

Reno

TRESPASSING ON 58

Horses stand asleep
White shadows cast in at their feet

      It's here that I saw you last fall

Lost in thought huge heads

      For one second

Turn as I pass between stalls
These vast barns house also
The owl and the moth

      My nostrils dilated in shock

The needling mosquito
Galloping rats

      Here I saw you

The drinker comes here
Furtive sighs
Float down from lofts

      Propped up with your back
      To a wall

A single rope hangs
From a beam

      Your legs
      Partly covered in straw

The spokes of the moon roll across the broad floor boards

      A light wind stirred
      In the six-feet-tall corn

Your forgotten face follows me back down the road

IN THE READING ROOM

Since I last looked up
from my book,
another appeared in the room
seated at the long table across from me
under the window,
bathed in gray light.

I don't think he has come
to reflect on the lyrics of Verlaine.

The one who with tremendous effort lifts his head
and stares straight at me, and sees nothing;
the one who suddenly gets to his feet
as though his name had been announced.

So far so good, no one has noticed.

Below the readers' faces,
set now in the impenetrable
cast of people sleeping,
pages go on turning
in the silence, so much snow
falling into a grave.

The one with head bent, eyelids closed,
looking at his hands.

THE EARTH WILL COME BACK FROM THE DEAD

Down empty roads gray with rain;
through branches
of new leaves then still
more light than leaf;
from turning alone, unperceived, with its sleeping, the wind
the transfiguring wind
in their leaves . . .
from turning, slowly
turning, turning
green
when everyone is gone.

BLOOD

My blood sits upright in a chair
its only thought, breath.

Though I walk around vacant,
inconsolable,
somebody's still breathing in me.

Mute, deaf and blind
yes—but someone
is still breathing
in me: the blood

which rustles and sleeps.
The suicide in me,
(the murderer).
The dreamer, the unborn.

But when I cut myself
I have to say:
this is my blood shed
for no one in particular.

If I get a nosebleed
I lie down on the cot, lie
there still, suspended
between the ceiling and floor

as though the bleeding
had nothing to do with me,
as though I'd been in an accident
but died one second before the collision.

In a hospital room
I have to turn my face
from the bright needle;
I see it, nevertheless,

and I see the blood,

and I see the test tube
in which my nurse carries it
obliviously, like a candle
in a sleepwalker's hand.

KNIFE

Holding a knife, or imagining it holds a knife, my blood goes to sleep in my fist. If I stare into it long enough, inevitably the moment when I no longer recognize it arrives. This is the moment when the blood unknowingly offers itself to be slaughtered; when cuts can occur like a slip of the tongue; when a little blood could billow in a glass of water and impart to it the disappearing taste of my own life.

MOSQUITOES

Playing your trumpets
thin as a needle
in my ear,
standing on my finger

or on the back of my neck
like the best arguments
against pity I know.
You insignificant vampires

that sip my life
through a straw;
you drops of blood
with wings;

carriers
of insomnia
I search for
with a lit match . . .

I had a job once
driving around in a truck
to look for your eggs.
They can be found

in ditches, near
train tracks, outside
of a barn
in an upright piano filled with rainwater.

It is impossible to kill
all of you,
invisible in the uncut grass
at the edges of the cemetery:

when the dogs go down there it
looks like they've gotten into birds.

DRINKING BACK

From where I am
I can hear the rain on the telephone
and the voices of nuns singing
in a green church in Brugge three years ago.

I can still see the hill,
the limestone fragment of an angel,
its mouth which has healed with
the illegible names in the cemetery,

the braillelike names—
the names of children, lovers, and the rest.
The names of people
buried with their watches running.

They are not sleeping, don't lie.

But it's true that once
every year of their death
it is spring.

INITIAL

To be able to say it: rose, oak, the stars . . .
and not to be blind!
Just to be here
for one day, only
to breathe and know when you lie down
you will keep on breathing;
to cast a reflection—,
oh, to have hands
even if they are a little damaged,
even if the fingers
leave no prints . . .

THE WISH

I'm tired of listening to these
conflicting whispers
before sleep;
I'm tired of this
huge, misshapen body.
I need another: and what could be prettier
than the wolf-spider's, with its small
hood of gray fur.
I'm told it can see in the dark;
I'm told how its children
spill from a transparent sack
it secretes, like a tear.
I know about its solitude,
ferocious and nocturnal . . .
I want to speak with this being.
I want it
to weave me a bridge.

THE VISIT

You're thinking of the pilot
in his glass cockpit
40,000 feet above the street
you live on
unseen
except for the white line
traced halfway across the darkening sky
all at once it dawns on you
the telephone is ringing
for the first time in weeks
and with equal suddenness
it ceases
as your hand goes to lift the receiver
in the next room
so that when you return to your window
the sky has grown empty the first stars

MORNING

A girl comes out
of the barn, holding
a lantern
like a bucket of milk

or like a lantern.
Her shadow's there.
They pump a bucket of water
and loosen their blouses,

they lead the mare out
from the field
their thin legs
blending with the wheat.

Crack a green kernel
in your teeth. Mist
in the fields,
along the clay road

the mare's footsteps
fill up with milk.

THE ROAD

I see the one walking this road
I see the one whose coat is thin whose shoes need mending
who is cold it's a very cold day
for stopping beside this dead cornfield
and basking one's face in those dark Rorschach clouds
I see the one whose lips say nothing
I see through his eyes I see the buried radiance in things
the one who isn't there

BRUSSELS, 1971

Some night
I will find myself walking
the sunlit halls of the school for the blind
I used to go past
on my way to the train
on my way to you gliding by one vacant classroom
after another all at once I will stop
inside the doorway
of one where a child
in white shirt and black tie sits
alone at a desk
fingertips pressed to the page
of an immense book
where leaves' shadows stir

and when I wake up
I will not remember
your face won't appear in my mind
and I will lie there a long time
hearing things
the pines outside a car
grinding its engine
a block away
the voice of a crow
this world's chilling star-rise
and I will open my eyes
and get it over with

POEM WITH NO SPEAKER
for Frank Stanford

Are you looking
for me? Ask that crow

rowing
across the green wheat.

See those minute air bubbles
rising to the surface

at the still creek's edge—
talk to the crawdad.

Inquire
of the skinny mosquito

on your wall
stinging its shadow,

this lock
of moon

lifting
the hair on your neck.

When the hearts in the cocoon
start to beat,

and the spider begins
its hidden task,

and the seed sends its initial
pale hairlike root to drink,

you'll have to get down on all fours

to learn my new address:
you'll have to place your skull

beside this silence
no one hears.

IN MEMORY
J. W.

I did not notice
it had grown dark as I sat there.

Needless to say,
speech no longer came
to your lips even soundlessly now.

You had been out for some time

when, in one slow unwilled motion,
your arm began to rise from the bed,

fingers spread, in a gesture resembling
the one you used to interrupt me,
that we might not miss
a particular passage of music.

from

Entry In An Unknown Hand (1989)

UNTITLED

Will I always be eleven,
lonely in this house,
reading books
that are too hard for me,
in the long fatherless hours.
The terrible hours of the window,
the rain-light
on the page,
awaiting the letter,
the phone call,
still your strange elderly child.

WINTER: TWILIGHT & DAWN

Buson said the winter rain
shows what is before our eyes
as though it were long ago.
I have been thinking about it for days,

and now I see.
And as I write the hills are turning green.
It does that here. The hills turn slowly
green in the interminable rain of late November,

as though time had begun
running backward
into a cold and unheard-of summer.
We are so far from you.

We are as far from you as stars, as those white
herons standing on the shore,
growing more distinct
as night comes—

What a black road this is.
Orion nailed there
upside down, and banking right
into the cloud and descending

behind Mt. Konocti.

(The week that marks the beginning
of my life marks
the beginning
of his death

the hour

ROOMS

Rooms I (I will not say
worked in) once heard in. Words
my mouth heard
then—be
with me. Rooms,
you open onto one
another: still house
this life, be in me
when I leave

THE CRAWDAD
for Dzvinia

The crawdad absorbed in minute excavations;
trees leaning over the water, the breathing
everywhere. And watching alone
a door I have walked through
into a higher
and more affectionate world—,
my face looking back at me, under the water
moss glowing faintly on stone.
We will not sleep, we will be changed.

JOSEPH COME BACK AS THE DUSK
(1950-1982)

The house is cold. It's raining,
getting dark. That's Joseph

for you: it's that time
of the day again.

We had been drinking, oddly enough.
He left.

I thought, a walk—
It's lovely to walk.

His book and glasses on the kitchen table.

QUANDARY
for Keith Hollaman

All day I slept
and woke and slept

again, the square
of winter sky lighting

the room,
which had grown

octaves
grayer.

What to do, if the words disappear as you write—
what to do

if they remain,
and you disappear.

TO THE HAWK

In the unshaded hill
where you kill
every day I have climbed
for a glimpse of you; below me
all the earth turned
golden
in the searing wind, the
wind itself golden, its abrupt blast
at a bend in the road
as I approach the summit, shining
wind, where you live
waiting to visit
its own Christless invisible blue and quite terminal instant
on some ex-jackrabbit, plummeting
upward, or floating
suspended
past sight-nimbus: closed eyes
beholding themselves in the sun.

AUDIENCE

The street deserted. Nobody,
only you and one last
dirt-colored robin,
clenching its branch
against the wind. It seems
you have arrived
late, the city unfamiliar,
the address lost.
And you made such a serious effort—
pondered the obstacles deeply,
tried to be your own critic.
Yet no one came to listen.
Maybe they came, and then left.
After you traveled so far,
just to be there.
It was a failure, that is what they will say.

ALCOHOL

You do look a little ill.

But we can do something about that, now.

Can't we.

The fact is you're a shocking wreck.

Do you hear me.

You aren't all alone.

And you could use some help today, packing in the
dark, boarding buses north, putting the seat back and
grinning with terror flowing over your legs through
your fingers and hair . . .

I was always waiting, always here.

Know anyone else who can say that.

My advice to you is think of her for what she is:
one more name cut in the scar of your tongue.

What was it you said, "To rather be harmed than
harm, is not abject."

Please.

Can we be leaving now.

We like bus trips, remember. Together

we could watch these winter fields slip past, and
never care again,

think of it.

I don't have to be anywhere.

At the End of the Untraveled Road

Under Konocti
the long eucalyptus-lined
road in the moon,
wind of November,
the now hawkless
hills
      turning green—
it was always here, not yet remembered.

Whatever it is

I was seeking, with my tactless despair:
it has already happened.
And I'm on my way now,
the pages too heavy to turn,
the first morning lights coming on
over the lake. How happy I am!
There's no hope for me.

VERMONT CEMETERY

Drowsy with the rain
and late October sun, remember,
we stopped to read the names.
A mile across the valley

a little cloud of sheep
disappeared over a hill,
a little crowd of sleep—
time to take a pill

and wake up,
and drive through the night.
Once I spoke your name,
but you slept on and on.

MORNING ARRIVES

Morning arrives
unannounced
by limousine: the tall
emaciated chairman

of sleeplessness in person
steps out on the sidewalk
and donning black glasses, ascends
the stairs to your building

guided by a German shepherd.
After a couple faint knocks
at the door, he slowly opens
the book of blank pages

pointing out
with a pale manicured finger
particular clauses,
proof of your guilt.

NORTH COUNTRY ENTRIES

Do you still know these early leaves, trans-
lucent, shining, spreading on their branches
like green flames.

And the hair-raising stars flowing over the
ridge late at night.

No one home in the house by itself on the
pine-hidden road,

or the 4-story barn up the road, leaning on
its hill.

The two horses who've opened the gate to their
field, old, wandering around on the lawn.

The sky becoming ominous.

Which is more awful, a sentient or endlessly
presenceless sky?

BIRTHDAY

I make my way down the back stairs
in the dark. I know
it sounds crude to admit it,
but I like to piss in the back yard.

You can be alone for a minute
and look up at the stars,
and when you return
everyone is there.

You get drunker, and listen to records.
Everyone agrees.
The dead singers have the best voices.
At four o'clock in the morning

the dead singers have the best voices.
And I can hear them now,
as I climb the stairs
in the dark I know.

THE NOTE
for C.D.

Summer is summer remembered;

a light on upstairs at the condemned orphanage,

an afternoon storm coming.

She heard a gun go off and one hair turned gray.

Somehow I will still know you.

THE TALK

Aged a lot during our talk
(you were gone).
Left and wandered the streets for some hours—
melodramatic, I know—
poor, crucified by my teeth.

And yet, how we talked
for a while.
All those things we had wanted to say for so long,
yes—I sat happily nodding
my head in agreement,
but you were gone.
In the end it gets discouraging.

I had let myself in;
I'd sat down in your chair.
I could just see you reading late
in the soft lamplight—
looking at a page,

listening to its voice:

yellow light shed in circles, in stillness,
all about your hair.

ILL LIT

Leaves stir overhead;
I write what I'm given to write.

The extension cord to the black house.

ENTRY IN AN UNKNOWN HAND

And still nothing happens. I am not arrested.
By some inexplicable oversight

nobody jeers when I walk down the street.

I have been allowed to go on living in this
room. I am not asked to explain my presence
anywhere.

What posthypnotic suggestions were made; and
are any left unexecuted?

Why am I so distressed at the thought of taking
certain jobs?

They are absolutely shameless at the bank—
you'd think my name meant nothing to them. Non-
chalantly they hand me the sum I've requested,

but I know them. It's like this everywhere—

they think they are going to surprise me: I,
who do nothing but wait.

Once I answered the phone, and the caller hung up—
very clever.

They think that they can scare me.

I am always scared.

And how much courage it requires to get up in the
morning and dress yourself. Nobody congratulates
you!

At no point in the day may I fall to my knees and
refuse to go on, it's not done.

I go on

dodging cars that jump the curb to crush my hip,

accompanied by abrupt bursts of black-and-white
laughter and applause,

past a million unlighted windows, peered out at
by the retired and their aged attack-dogs—

toward my place,

the one at the end of the counter,

the scalpel on the napkin.

DURATION

On the sill
the blown-out candle

burning
in the past.

Frozen clouds
passing over

the border
north. Listen

to the end,
listen with me.

No Longer Or Not Yet
(from a phrase by Hermann Broch)

In the gray temples of business

In the famine of the ant-bewitched seed

Wolves attacking people in the half-deserted suburbs

And kings dead with their hands crossed on their genitals
                a thousand years from now

In sunlight shining on your vacant place at the table

In the sneer and the kick in the face world without end

In my crouched shadow loping beside me

In the imbecilic prose of my thoughts

In the voice of the one fingerprinted blindfolded and shot

World of dead parents unconsciously aped without end

In the hand above the rainbow horses of the Peche-Merle cave walls

We interrupt this program to bring you the announcement
                that enemy ICBMs will begin to arrive in
                ten minutes

In the strangeness which corridors and stairwells have for children

Death of the weekday

In their parties alone in a sip from an empty cup

In the little grass toad beating in your palm

The spider spinning in the dust the barren worm

The death of tears

In the gashed vivid colors of gas station restrooms at
                three in the morning

(And we thank Thee for destroying the destroyers of the
        world)

In the unaccompanied boy on the Greyhound the old woman
        with a balloon

World no longer or not yet

The moon which goes dragging the ocean and turning
        its chalky steppes away

Unsummonable world

In the white stars in the black sky shining in the past

The black words in the white page uttered long ago

Death of tears

In the storm of wordless voices the hand abruptly
        shocked into dictation

(Envelop me clothe me in blackness book closed)

In early March crocuses pushing deafly through soil

While you quietly turn between dreams like a page

The morning light standing in the room like someone
        who has returned after long absence
        younger

World no longer or not yet

LOOK INTO ITS EYES

The leaved wind,

the leaved wind
in the mirror

and windows, perceived
by the one-week-old.

Forever, we weren't here—

THE DAY

My mother picks me up at school.
Strange. I leave the others playing,
walk to where she's parked—
and why are we driving so slowly?

You have to turn right here, she whispers.
When we get there the whole house is silent.
Why's that? Does this mean
I can watch The Three Stooges?

Evidently. She's driving away now
and he is not typing downstairs:
he isn't there at all, I've checked.
This must be my lucky day.

NIGHT WRITING

The sound of someone crying in the next apartment.

In an unfamiliar city, where I find myself once
more

unprepared for this specific situation

or any situation whatsoever, now—

frozen in the chair,

my body one big ear.

A big ear crawling up a wall.

In the room where I quietly rave and gesticulate—
and no one must hear me—
alone until sleep:

my life a bombed site turning green again.

The sound of someone crying

THERE
(Thomas Frank)

Let it start to rain,
the streets are empty now.
Over the roof hear the leaves
coldly conversing in whispers;
a page turns in the book
left open by the window.
The streets are empty, now
it can begin.

Like you
I wasn't present
at the burial. This morning

I have walked out
for the first time
and wander here
among the blind
flock of names
standing still
in the grass—

(the one on your stone
will remain
listed in telephone books
for a long time, I guess, light
from a disappeared star . . .)

—just to locate the place,
to come closer, without knowing where you are
or if you know I am there.

POEM

for Frank Bidart

Per each dweller
one grass blade, one leaf
one apartment
one shadow
one rat.

By itself, defending a lost position,

the poem
          writing the poet . . .

Anvil of solitude

So diminish the city's population
by one, and go
add your tear to the sea—

Heart that wonderfully lasted
                         until
I learned how to write
what it so longed to say

Nothing of the kind.

A DAY COMES

A day comes
when it has always been winter,
will always be winter.
Witnesses said the crowd fled
through the park, chased by policemen on horseback
past the Tomb of the Unknown
Celebrity as the guard
was being changed,
but they are gone.
The witnesses are gone.
A day comes
when the planet stops turning.
It is February here,
late afternoon.
It will always be late afternoon,
neither dark nor light out.
But we cannot be bothered,
because we are asleep;
the door is locked.
Now and then somebody comes and knocks
and goes away again
back down the hall,
back down the stairs.
But we cannot be bothered,
because we are asleep
and listening,
listening.
Do you hear the wind?
We have always been asleep,
will always be asleep—
turning over
like pages on fire . . .
Where were we?
We were listening.
No, I don't hear it either.
The wind, the marching
boots, the burning
names.

THREE DISCARDED FRAGMENTS
From the notebooks of Rilke

Who can say, when I go to a window,
that someone near death doesn't
turn his eyes in my direction
and stare and, dying, feed on me.
That in this very building the forsaken
face isn't lifted, that needs me now

*

That smile, for a long time
he couldn't describe it—
the velvet depression
left by a jewel . . .

*

A child's soul like a leaf light still shines through

THE STREET

On it lives one bird

who commences singing, for some reason best
known to itself, at precisely 4 a.m.

Each day I listen for it in the night.

I too have a song to say alone,

but can't begin. On it, surrounded by blocks of
black warehouses,

is located this room. I say this room, but no
one knows

how many rooms I have. So many rooms how will I
light

This isn't working out, is it

Here's what really occurred, in my own words.

I murdered my father—and if he comes back I'll kill him again—but
first I persuaded him to abandon my mother. Now you know. It was
me all along. Then I got bored, held a knife to her throat and made
her marry the sadist who tortured my brother for ten years.

I feel bad about it, but what can I do.

I mean we're talking about a genetic predisposition here.

I *am* taking my medication. And things have gotten a lot better.

And if I ever finish writing this, I'm going to tear that bird's head off
and eat it.

MY WORK

For Jordy and Linda Powers

The way I work is strange.

For one thing, you would never call it work.

Although I'm good at that.

Work is not the term.

It destroys me, I adore it—

I'll look at it someday and noticing its utility
still fails to surpass that of a lyre locked up in
a glass case tuned an octave above human hearing,

I'll take an ax to it.

I'll stop speaking to it.

I'll sit alone in some shit-hole and inject it
until the jewels roll out of my eyes.

I don't know what all I'll do,

snow of
        unlit afternoon . . .

mute and agreed-to
descent

COORDINATES

Waking up at an improbable hour
in the small gray-lit apartment
where I can never bring myself
to believe I actually live;
going off in the winter morning to teach
certain there's been a mistake,
knowing as I enter the classroom
the students will look in my face
with unanimous amusement
and lack of recognition,
that before I can utter a word
someone in a suit will appear
and ask me to come with him.

*

This won't hurt at all.
It does?
Well we haven't been taking good care of them
have we. Difficulty explaining to some
the concept of financial terror—
specifically, that if you're afraid to buy food
if you can help it you are not going to spend
$1500 on a tooth;
difficulty of explaining anything
with your mouth clamped open.
Under anesthesia

I walk along a sunflower field I know of

*

It was still day
when I boarded the train.

The tunnel

then the Charles,
and soft blue lights of traffic in the rain.

*

Everyone in his right mind is asleep.
A black car glides past,
in its wake (the

speed blossoming coldly

through fingers and spine)
a prolonged Coltrane scream

and a shiver of beauty open the night

WAITING UP

I can remember you
mentioning once
how you'd wait until your mother was preoccupied
or gone, to dress
the doll all in white
for its little funeral—
how all the while it stared into your eyes
with its cold unbeckonable eyes,
and seemed to smile.
Why this
I couldn't say. And then again
why not? It's easy
to remember anything.
I'll walk now, maybe.
The clouds' stature slumbrously building
and blooming on the horizon,
identityless, huge
gesticulations from the trees,
the bird's voice
hidden back in the leaves,
the remote barely audible wake
from the roar of an airliner's engines
fill the dim morning.
Maybe your presence
will startle me now;
maybe I'll rise from
this chair.
Maybe the room will be empty.

The room will be empty,
and you will not come.

GUESTS

Smell of winter pine trees in the air;
around me night, the wind, Marie, the stars.
Last night I dreamed I stood here,
this very spot—why I've come—
lights on in a house across the valley
where there is no house.
Stood here as I lay beside you
and looked so fondly at those lights
they might have been our home, and why not?
Everyone you see
lives somewhere.
How is this done?

WINTER ENTRIES

Love no one, work, and don't let the pack know you're
wounded . . .

Stupid, disappointed strategies.

Hazel wind of dusk, I have lived so much.

Friendless eeriness of the new street—

The poem does not come, but its place is kept set.

GOING NORTH IN WINTER

The sound of pines in the wind.
And to think you're the only person on earth
isn't hard, at the end
of the long journey nowhere.
Yet in the end I have come to
love this room and be the one
looking out on snowfields, blank
scores of wire fence in the deepening
snow, the wind through them a passage
of remembered music, bare
unbeckoning branches
with never a ghost
of a deciduous rustling,
the stilled river
with the sheet over its face . . .
going north in winter.
And it's all right
to glance out the window:
the fear will grow less
or more intense, but
it will always be there. Unseen
it's a palpable force,
isn't it. Like electricity
which can be employed,
as has been pointed out,
to kill you in a chair
or light your room.
But I'm through with that now.
I reach over and switch on the dark.
It's all right to pronounce a few words
when you're by yourself, and feel a little joy.

from

The Night World and the Word Night (1993)

ILLEGIBILITY

Hawk in golden space

Thick-leaved, darkly
beckoning trees
bigger than the house

Sunlit apparitional
peaks of a thunderhead
fading
to the east

Page
from conception to death mask

The stranger who approaches on the
       street and says, You
       don't remember me

OCCURRENCE

I've gotten everyone who hurt me.

In a blackout a man loads his shotgun
again.

Outside the genuine star spangled twilight
of North Dakota
unfurls, twinkling and barking.

The *he* becomes a ghost.

Big windblown rags of bitching crows
resettle
in the trees out back.

PAWTUCKET POSTCARDS

Neon sign missing a letter

Firearm with an obliterated serial number

There's always death
But getting there—
you can't just say the word

Rhode Island Artificial Limb Co.

Lights of the abandoned
households reflected
in the little river through the leaves

The posthistoric clouds

LONELINESS

Say you wake
in the night
abruptly alone
in the midst of addressing
vast stadiums . . .

Or at an intersection windows
shattered your forehead
leaning on the horn
a crowd materializing a light
snow beginning

Like the taste of alcohol to children

No

That with which there is nothing to compare

Say you have no friends, or
say you have to go to sleep

To see your friends

There

It's not so bad
the stitches itch
where they removed
your rage
is all

Where they removed
those thoughts

And no one
misses *them*

After several weeks
everyone learns
how to tie his own shoe

You get a little doll that looks like you

WORDS

I don't know where they come from.
I can summon them
(sometimes I can)
into my mind,
into my fingers,
I don't know why. Or I'll suddenly hear them
walking, sometimes
waking—
they don't often come when I need them.
When I need them most terribly,
never.

GONE

I dreamed you came and sat beside me
on the bed

It was something that you had
to tell me

I dreamed you came and sat beside me

Like a drowning at a baptism

Like an embittered shopper returning

The sad misspelled obscenities on men's room walls

Snow on dark water . . . something

CERTAIN TALL BUILDINGS

I know a little
about it: I know
if you contemplate suicide
long enough, it
begins to contemplate you—
oh, it has plans for you.
It calls to your attention

the windows of certain tall
buildings, wooded snow fields
in your memory where you might cunningly vanish
to remotely, undiscoverably
sleep. Remember your mother
hanging the cat
in front of you when you were four?

Why not that? That
should fix her. Or deep drugs
glibly prescribed by psychiatrists weary
as you of your failure to change
into someone else—
you'll show them
change.

These thoughts, occurring once too often,
are no longer your own. No,
they think you.
The thing is not to entertain them
in the first place, dear
life, friend.
Don't leave me here without you.

AUGUST INSOMNIA

He slowly replaced the receiver
like somebody who had just used it.

He slowly replaced the receiver
like somebody who had just used it
to strike himself
hard,
several times,
on the skull.

Midnight, blue leaves swarming against the glass.

The pregnant child alone on her front doorstep,

the starving moon.

He slowly replaced the receiver.

JAMAIS VU

Whether I grow old, betray my dreams, become a ghost

or die in flames
like Gram,
like Frank,
like Thomas James—

I think for a while I'll come back
as a guest to a childhood room
where the sun is the sun once again
and the wind in the trees is the wind
in the trees, and the summer afternoon
the endless summer afternoon
of books,
that only happiness . . .

I won't have written this.

Smell of leaves before rain, green

light that shines not
on, but from the
earth—

for me, too,

a hunger darkened the world
and a fierce joy made it blaze
into unrecognizable beauty.

NIGHT SAID

I lay on my back in the yard,
my face among the stars.
Night said, don't go inside.
There's murder in the house,
but that is far away;
don't answer when they call.

They used to call and call,
but it was so dark in the yard.
And I had gone so far away—
guided by the stars
I could set out from the burning house
and watch them sink inside.

I tried to stay inside,
thinking perhaps you would call,
cause silence in the shrieking house:
if I were in the yard
the voice behind the stars
might never find the way;

plus you can't be out there always.
You are compelled to come inside
at some point, leave the stars
abruptly when a strange man calls
your name into the long black yard,
obey the catastrophic house.

I knew I had a real house,
with a real father, a ways—
some states—beyond that yard.
I was a happy child, inside.
Until my name was called
I lay on my back filling with stars,

I raised my hand amid the stars.
Tumultuous leaves hid the bright nightmare house.
Happy and evil for a moment, I called
drop H-bomb here—a little ways
from me, a bird spoke once. Inside
someone flung open the door to my yard,

but called my name into an empty yard.
By now the house was only one more star—
unwithstandable inside, but just a jewel-light far away.

THE WORLD

Mood-altering cloud of late autumn

Gray deserted street

Place settings for one—dear visible things . . .

The insane are right, but they're still the insane.

While there is time let me a little belong.

THE FORTIES

And in the desert cold men invented the star

UNTITLED

I basked in you;
I loved you, helplessly, with a boundless tongue-tied love.
And death doesn't prevent me from loving you.
Besides,
in my opinion you aren't dead.
(I know dead people, and you are not dead.)

THE LOVERS

Who knows but before their closed eyes
both faces change
in slow reverse

recapitulation
of the faces
each has never seen again:

fetally then
full-blown, in a moment
taking on the different

features of their secret
genealogies
of lovers,

until each has the face
that first troubled the other's
and both sleep with a stranger in their arms.

UNTITLED

This was the first time I knelt
and with my lips, frightened, kissed
the lit inwardly pink petaled lips.

It was like touching a bird's exposed heart
with your tongue.

Summer dawn flowing into the room parting the
curtains—the lamp dimming—breeze

rendered visible. Lightning,
                              and then soft applause
from the leaves . . .

Almost children, we lay asleep in love listening to the
rain.

We didn't ask to be born.

SAY MY NAME

I'd be entombed
inside a period

in the closed book
in the huge dark

of St. Paul's
where we used to meet,

                wafted

downaisle toward
banked sunlight-colored candles.

I'd be in your mouth,
in that huger dark:

body that stands for the soul.

Word that means you are loved.

FOR MARTHA

You are the bright yellow spider who hides in the apricot
leaves, watching me work.

You are the redwood shade pouring down around me in
blond columns, and you are the air

coolly and goldenly
scented

as the certainty of sleep
when I lie down weary

and at peace, and as the certainty that I will rise again

sane and refreshed—. . .

And my bright yellow spider hiding in the apricot leaves

FOR A FRIEND WHO DISAPPEARED

Just one more time. Only one—
the small rose of blood blooming in the syringe—
one to compel haunted speech to the lips,
sure. Some immense seconds pass. Dusk's
prow slowly glides right up Avenue B;
the young Schumann's two personalities
continue discussing each other
in the diary. Your eyes
move to the warning
on a pack of cigarettes—
good thing you're not pregnant!
Still no speech, but no pain either,
no New York,
nothing,
sweet.
You happen to know that you're home.
And how simple it was, and how smart
to come back: in the moon
on its oak branch
the owl slowly opens
its eyes like a just severed head
that hears its name called out,
and spreads its wings
and disappears;
and the moth leaves the print
of its lips on the glass, lights
on the lamp's stillwarm bulb,
the napper's forehead,
his hand, where it rests
down the chair arm,
fingers
slowly opening.

UNTITLED

Sicklemoon between thunderheads in the
blue of four in the afternoon

And when the first star occurred to the sky—. . .

Why did one write
such things. Not
to describe them—
they don't need us to describe them.
But to utter them
into existence,

just as they *looked at us*
into existence . . .

Oh to give back to them
the existence perceiving them
bestows on us—

just to say them:

to say and feel said,
feel somehow at home here.

TIME TO STOP KEEPING A DREAM JOURNAL

This time I dreamed I was writing a dream down

And later on that gray April morning—an out-of-
the-house experience!—

the cemetery blanketed with robins

I held my shadow's hand (he leadeth me)

Hour when each human reports
to the mirror

Leafprints in the sidewalk
unidentified flowering
lavender shrubs
in an otherwise black-and-white
landscape, I pass
through an evil rainbow

A pair of glasses found in a pile of dead leaves: one
of the stations of my day

(Orders, orders, orders: yes, Your Absence—no, Your
Nonexistence . . .)

And inevitable night again 1 a.m. leaves' sounds the
empty moth still clinging to the screen

Shape of leaf mouth eye—the spider in the iris—

And the great trees rustle the moon staring into the
sockets in the grass

And 2 o'clock streets filled with teenagers in fascist drag

And in five years you'll see them collecting at bus stops
like dust

And still the hand will sleep in its glass ship—. . .

MIDNIGHT POSTSCRIPT
for my friend Joseph Kahn:
born 1950, drowned 1982

Walking the floor after midnight
I leaf through your pharmacopoeia
or a book on stars.

How I love the night.

It should always be
night, and the living with their TVs, vacuum cleaners
and giggling inanities
silenced.

With here and there a window lit a low golden mysterious
                              light.

I love the night world,
                    the word night.
Book & door. Joseph. Death's leaves—. . .

I'm never going to get this right.

And I can't go on forming
and tasting your name
or biting down in blinding pain
forever—no,

from now on I have entered
                              and live in our unspoken words.

And the space I took up in the world scarlessly closes like water.

THE WINTER SKYLINE LATE

I walk, neverendingly
walk

hating the rain

the odd million gray disgraced
looks you will meet on the subways
                                    the streets

everything
that will hurt you today . . .

As I have walked these after midnight
streets so many
years, unwelcome and alone

stopping a minute at some frozen payphone

gagged on my pride
                        and moved on

                Moonset, dawn:
Konocti

                Venus-lit
greenish horizon

apples
        shadow-dappled
in the early wind . . .

It might have been, somehow

Not now

Eating fear, shitting fear, convulsed
with tedium and horror
every time I went
                        to touch a pen to paper

Crying
in a downtown porno theater

But in our eyes we are never lost

Looking at the skyline, late
some see the site of triumphant
far off celebrations
to which they weren't invited
some see a little light
left on for them
and some
the final abrupt unendurable radiance
blooming

Local bar of deceased revelers

Special subway station for distinguished lunatics

Cold stars beyond the Charles,
                              ward of bandaged eyes
that turn and stare in my direction as I pass

Black wind and distant lights
I prayed
that I might disappear

Unfather, unsay me
I asked
irreparably here

But why are we drawn walking at night
to certain unfamiliar
solitary places
                    Why
this interest in a stranger's lights
Whose ghosts are we

What happened to our faces

The wind moves slowly, fingers
read my forehead
eyelids
lips

The constant sight
of what might have been
aged them
Their million mute
unnoticed acts of insubordination
and inconsequential
cruelty aged them—

Yellow window
in the blue dawn
lost is lost
and gone is gone but
be there
if I wake again, don't abandon me
defend me

CLEARLAKE OAKS (I)

Konocti's summit
sunlit
on the other shore . . .

To sleep in the mountain
(when have I
ever slept) blissfully
sown

through an infinite imageless brightness—

inspected and forgotten by a grass green dragonfly.

CLEARLAKE OAKS (II)

The hawk rises
into the sun;
the lizard goes testing the dust
with its tongue—

stationary
hour, above
the windless
blond and shadow of the hill.

And I am
here to say this,

my mysterious
privilege and joy.

THE DRUNK

I don't understand any more
than you do. I only know
he stays here
like some huge wounded animal—
open the door and he will gaze at you and
      linger
Close the door
and he will break it down

THE ANGEL (I)

in memory of Marguerite Young

Decay of a tone, decay of the sun

Green eyes unseen among the leaves

The reader's lips
                     the dreamer's lids

Moon dissolving under the tongue

                Messenger
from a word a noun
with an imaginary corresponding
entity in space

              The human
face about to come

                Midnight's
world-altering
name

And someone gives birth to a child

And laboring someone
gives death to himself

The objects in the room lit up with pain

THE ANGELS (II)

No one loves them because they are ugly

They are ugly because no one loves them . . .

One of the racists of beauty

I feel three green voices
                              gazing at me—

My very existence
inexpiable—

the gardener at the tomb

THEORY

What do I care about
walking erect,

the fingers freed
to clutch large sticks, the hand
to hide behind the back—

bared teeth
slowly learning to form
an expression of welcome and pleasure . . .

Man was born
when an animal wept.

THE DOOR

Going to enter the aged horizontal cellar door

(the threshing leaves, the greenish light
of the approaching storm)

you suddenly notice you're opening the cover of an
enormous book.

One that's twice as big as you are—

but you know all about that:

the groping descent alone in total darkness,

toward—what?

You know what you're looking for, and you forget; and
maybe you have no idea

yet. But you know something is down there, and a
light you need to find

before you can even begin to search . . .

THOUGHTS OF A SOLITARY FARMHOUSE

And not to feel bad about dying.
Not to take it so personally—

it is only
the force we exert all our lives

to exclude death from our thoughts
that confronts us, when it does arrive,

as the horror of being excluded—. . .
something like that, the Canadian wind

coming in off Lake Erie
rattling the windows, horizontal snow

appearing out of nowhere
across the black highway and fields like billions of white bees.

TIDEPOOL: ELK, CALIFORNIA

Skirting such thick undulating underwater
hair, the invisible

crevice haunting eel,
the hand-like crab

and moon-dilated anemones,
I remember

hunting the tremendous boulders'
undersides—, how then

armed with these
long knives we pried

the abalone's
unrelenting

nursing
from its stone.

1969

UNTITLED
for E.

I have to sleep to think sometimes—
waking into sleep
where you find a world reversed, your blindness
hearing . . .
as the tedious prose of the world disappears
on its ruined page leaving nothing
but the effortlessness of a window
looking out on
the unsayable mystery
saying itself;
text one has long sought to translate,
even if poorly, only to read it—
here for some moments
weirdly improved on.
Without wearing out one's knees
or gnashing of teeth
or pulling out of hair
or disappointment, or terror
but with a return
to the original
gratitude:
as once at 15
for perhaps half an hour—
I remember and await.

ELEGY: BREECE D'J PANCAKE

We can always be found
seated at a bar
the glass before us
empty, with our halos
of drunk flies—
or standing
in the dark across the street
from the Sacramento
Coroner's. (And my friend
we're all in there
floating along
the ceiling, tethered
to our laughing gas canisters.) We are
old people shopping,
next winter's ghosts,
the prostitute
in her mortician's make-up
strolling York Avenue at 3 a.m.,
the fellow in Atlantic City
furtively pawning a doll.
Quick suture,
lightning,
hush-finger—
cheap eeriness of wind chimes—
summer thunder
from a cloudless sky . . .
The abandoned abandon.
There are no adults.
You're dead
but look who's talking.

THE SPIDER

For a long time I was attracted
to small things. Spiders
particularly: the spiders
who lived in my house

were simply not to be found
although I didn't want to
torture them. It's true
I might have frightened some

in my sleep, I might have
stepped on one without
seeing it, friendly. I did
see one once

but it ran off
very quickly, like a man
who notices a large
crowd coming forward to stone him.

Something about the thin shadow
of a nail in the wall;
the trees' shadows
moving on the bed

while a being casts its
two inches of vision
from a remote corner of the ceiling
into the room . . .

Once, at dawn, when I was sick
I went through the house
with my drug-lit eyes,
I stopped by the window

and sat down at the piano
in order to type something
about your childhood:
a sip from an empty cup

a doll cemetery.
A spider appeared, creeping
toward my fingers
like a little furry hand.

I lie down,
I press the place behind my ear
where the vein is.
Today

I observe the absence
of my brother
sentience: the spider
who lived in my room

with its minute blood.

BILD, 1959

As the bourbon's level
descended in the bottle
his voice would grow
lower and more
indistinct, like a candle flame
under a glass

Sunlight in the basement room

So he reads to me
disappearing
When he is gone

I go over
and secretly taste his drink

Mushroom cloud of sunset

TRAIN NOTES

Voicing
in itself
was the allowing to appear
of that which the voicing one saw
because it once looked into him . . .

Green desuetude of railroad
tracks, wild
apples, aging limestone
angel's face and
changing
cloud

Green lightning past the last trees, they are pure gaze

I am wandering through the corridors of a deserted
                                        elementary school

I am flying
            over a dark sea

Jolted awake
I meet my own eyes
staring back from badly executed features

(Like a scar the face speaks for itself)

But irises, iris—a meteor,
chrysalis, a woman's
name, a flower's
sentient light

Green eye the altering light alters

Unlit
        until the sun

Damned to language, we come from the sun

From stars and weather flowing in opposite directions
Stars slowly silently flowing
and setting,
beginningless

from

Rorschach Test (1995)

VOICE

I woke up at 4 in the afternoon. Rain woke
me. Dark. Mail—a voice said, You'll have
mail,

scaring and gladdening my heart. Enough anyway
to get it to leave the bed, attempt to make coffee,
dress and begin limping downstairs. All

the boxes were empty. Of course. A voice said,
He just hasn't come yet. But I knew: it is 4
in the afternoon—the others have already taken

the mail indoors. Hours ago. If this my box
is empty now then it was always empty.

Rain. Darker

now. By the time I had walked, more or less,
back up the stairs, the treacherous voice had
nothing more to say.

Hope. They call it hope—

that obscene cruelty, it never lets up for a
minute.

But not anymore—never again. If the telephone
rings just don't answer it, said the voice. Very
adaptable, the obsequious voice. If the mail does
come put it in the garbage with its fellow trash;
or set it on fire in that big metal can in the alley,
you know, your publisher. Dark. Odd. It was
light when I finally slept, I hear myself saying so
out loud. I suppose I am insane again,

on top of everything else. He talks to himself now,
they'll say. Who. By the time you get back to your
room you won't even exist. A bit mean now. And you
will sit down in the chair with your back to the
window, it observes.

After a little I know for a fact you will open your
notebook and write all this down,

why I don't know. No doubt you will even show it to
somebody, at some point: they'll talk to you, offer advice,

admit admiration for this phrase,

dislike for that. But they don't understand. You don't

care now—how can you. No, I don't care what they say,
what they do to me now. I used to. Terribly. And then you didn't.

And then I didn't.

INFANT SEA TURTLES

Think of them setting out from their enormous beached eggs
to follow the moon to the sea
and into the sea.

Think of them hatching, so strange—
like some misshapen birds who haven't yet grown wings.
But no, they are far in advance of that, returning

to the sea that vast tear we came crawling out of.
Led there by what we call the moon:
Eve, or caesarean child.

The moon which left the great scar called the sea
when it tore itself from the earth's side
and flung itself out into space,

lover or child, to escape—but not far enough—. . .

THE COMEDIAN

I was mad when I got home
and smelled the alcohol.
I thought he was sleeping, though
the color of the skin, the
breathing and the drool were strange.

Impossible to touch him or get near.
He started, as I guess
I sort of barked at him through tears.
All I asked for was an ambulance
I'm sure, though don't remember phoning. Cops

searched for drugs in my empty film canisters.
Nobody really saw *me*.
The "Final Wish," as he put it
in the almost illegible note that was pinned
to the wall like a crucifix over the head

of the bed of some lonely serious child:
something having to do with cremation
and scattering ashes on the Ohio. And do you know
I laughed. I actually laughed—what does he think this is—
left by myself in the house. It was a scream.

HEAVEN

There is a heaven.

These sunflowers—those dark, wind-threshed
oaks—. . .

Heaven's all around you,

though getting there is hard:

it is death,
heaven.

But they are only words.

ONE IN THE AFTERNOON

Unemployed, you take a walk.
At an empty intersection
you stop to look both ways as you were taught.
An old delusion coming over you.
The wind blows through the leaves.

BEGINNING OF NOVEMBER

The light is winter light.
You've already felt it
before you can open your eyes,
and now it's too late
to prepare yourself
for this gray originless
sorrow that's filling the room. It's not winter. The light
is. The light is
winter light,
and you're alone.
At last you get up:
and suddenly notice you're holding
your body without the heart
to curse its lonely life, it's suffering
from cold and from the winter
light that fills the room
like fear. And all at once you hug it tight,
the way you might hug
somebody you hate,
if he came to you in tears.

THE MEETING

I happened to be in a strange city
drinking.
One of those dives where you enter
and just pull the covers over your head;
where the gentleman sitting five inches away
has lately returned from his mission in space
in the one coeducational toilet stall
existing on the premises,
and will continue to sit there forever, nodding
and peering down into his shot-glass
like a man struggling to keep awake over a bombsight;
and the aged transsexual
whore who never got around
to the final operation in his youth
seems to be pursing her lips
in your direction, demurely, down bar.
One of those places with windows
the color of your glasses—
a fact which in no way compels you
to remove them. Nobody cares
about your eyes: they'll go on serving you
as long as you can talk,
as long as you can still pronounce
your drink by name and are tactful
enough not to fall off your stool
or call anyone's attention
to the fetus in the vodka bottle
to the left of the vast Bartender's
silent, "Another?"
It was then you walked past,
outside the window, unhindered
by the event's complete impossibility.
This kind of thing's happened to everyone.
No? Never mind, then:
I will describe it.
At whichever ground zero
you've found yourself waiting, waiting,
there is one and only one person
whose sudden dumbfounding appearance
could, if not exactly save you,
afford you some respite
from the slightly green outpatient
you're supposed to be keeping an eye on there
behind the beverages in the mirror, the one

whose job is watching you . . .
Then she walks by.
Though the instant this transpires
you know it's already too late,
she's vanished right back again
into one of those infinite places
where you are not. And it's pointless
to run to the door, tear it open and scream
her name into the freezing wind:
it doesn't stand a chance
of being heard above
the amused roar of the sky's numberless sports fans.
No—you need a strategy.
Needless to say, this calls for a drink or ten.
Now this individual, her special haunts:
there is still a very slight chance
they are all in your mind, the grim city
that's changed somewhat since you've been here
attending your dark little party.
And God knows what's happened to the one
outside the door, a place
you have never really been to
and one where you never intended
to do a lot of sightseeing.
You are a peaceful man.
But what can you do—time's passing faster,
and your loneliness is ruined anyway.
You down your shot of fear and hit the street.

LATE LATE SHOW

Undressing, after working all night,
the last thing I see is the room

in the house next door.
At 4 in the morning, a dark room

filled with that flickering
blue

so familiar, almost maternal
if you were born

in my generation:
this light

so small, reassuring you
that the world is still there

filled with friendly and beautiful people, people
who would like to give you helpful products—

adoring families—
funny Nazis . . .

            Undressing, the
last thing I will see.

HEROIN

And now it's gone
I'll wait
for time to come
and tuck me in

a little white blank
envelope,

and mail me
on this pretty wind-lights

midnight:
I am safe

here in the darkness,
the gloating

vampire
of myself,

waiting for the sudden light
to open, its enormous hand

to sort me from the others
and to raise me up
and finding me spotless, devoid
of destination or origin,

transport me
to the painless fire
of permanent, oblivious
invisibility.

RORSCHACH TEST

To tell you the truth I'd have thought it had gone out of use long ago;
there is something so 19th-century about it,

with its absurd reverse Puritanism.

Can withdrawal from reality or interpersonal commitment be gauged
by uneasiness at being summoned to a small closed room to discuss
ambiguously sexual material with a total stranger?

Alone in the presence of the grave examiner, it soon becomes clear
that, short of strangling yourself, you are going to have to find a way
of suppressing the snickers of an eight-year-old sex fiend, and feign cu-
riosity about the process to mask your indignation at being placed in
this situation.

Sure, you see lots of pretty butterflies with the faces of ancient Egypt-
ian queens, and so forth—you see other things, too.

Flying stingray vaginas all over the place, along with a few of their
male counterparts transparently camouflaged as who knows what pil-
lars and swords out of the old brain's unconscious.

You keep finding yourself thinking, "God damn it, don't tell me that
isn't a pussy!"

But after long silence come out with, "Oh, this must be Christ trying
to prevent a large crowd from stoning a woman to death."

The thing to do is keep a straight face, which is hard. After all, you're
supposed to be crazy

(and are probably proving it).

Maybe a nudge and a chuckle or two wouldn't hurt your case. Yes,

it's some little card game you've gotten yourself into this time, when
your only chance is to lose. Fold,

and they have got you by the balls—

just like the ones you neglected to identify.

REUNION

Movement of the hour hand, dilating
of the rose . . .
Once I could write those.
What am I? A skull

biting its fingernails, a no one
with nowhere to be
consulting his watch,
a country music station left on quietly

all night, the motel door left open
to Wheeling's rainy main street, the river
and wind
and every whisky-breathed

ghost in the family—
left open,
old man,
for you.

DEPICTION OF CHILDHOOD
After Picasso

It is the little girl
guiding the minotaur
with her free hand—
that devourer

and all the terror he's accustomed to
effortlessly emanating,
his ability to paralyze
merely by becoming present,

entranced somehow, and transformed
into a bewildered
and who knows, grateful
gentleness . . .

and with the other hand
lifting her lamp.

NIGHT WATERING

A big velvet-brown moth
with an eye on each wing, asleep
right in the middle of
the sunflower, its antennae stirring
lightly now and then. We are alone
on this dim barely window-lit street . . .
stirring, maybe because of the light
breeze or a semi-attentiveness
to my presence in its trance,
an inability to decide
if something's really there,
combined with a total indifference
since it has found at last its golden
temple of the myriad gold chambers
and its god. The flower
has virtually tripled in size
since bursting into bloom a week ago, in fact
it's grown so huge it is in danger
of breaking its own neck.
(It reminds me of someone we know.)
I spend about an hour
rummaging around the back porch
for twine and poles and so forth—it's beginning
to get blue out now—and finally
manage to prop up its head
so it will be comfortable.
At this point I am beginning
to appreciate the cool, still night
and it is almost gone. Now the moth
all this time has not budged
from its spot, it will not be disturbed
at its devotions. I stand in my own
fascination and envy, more
difficult to break at this point . . .
At last I return
to the house from this four o'clock watering—
happy for once
to have something important to tell you
when you wake up, when I
lie watching while the golden
petals of your eyes begin stirring, then
startlingly open
all-pupil, meet mine
and cannot decide what I am
or if I'm really there.

PLANES

Dream clock—next port of entry—. . .

By diurnal moonlight, by dream clock, by star-blueprint
it approaches

.

Over here they are sharpening
the seeing-eye
knife,
etc.

.

Her hand on my

shoulder
without a name

.

Tempus fuckit

.

Funny, I sometimes feel like a motherless child (trad.)
too, unknown
black voice

.

Friends never met

.

Put in the dark
to hear no lark

.

Heart with a miner's face

.

Poem, my afterlife

Blue underwater statuary

And when the sky gives up its dead . . .

        ·

Thank you, I've just received yours

Unless all these years
I've been misunderstanding

the verses. In any event

I'll scratch your back,
you knife mine

        ·

And when the sky gives up its dead

And when the dead rise blind and groping
around for scattered bones, the skulls
they don like helmets
before setting out, bumping into one another sadly
as they hoarsely cry
the full name
of some only friend

UNTITLED

The unanswering cold, like a stepfather
to a silent child

And the light
if that's what it is

The steplight

No—

the light that's always leaving

THE FAMILY'S WINDY SUMMER NIGHT

The moon on her shoulder
like skin—
brightest and nightest desire.
Her eyes, unknown to him,
wide open. Dark
for dark's sake, he recalls:
the fallacy still
unavoidable.
Child,
the glass of sleep
unasked for and withheld.

THE LEAVES

I have been sitting here
all of the past
hour very sleepily watching the wind
as it blows through the black leaves
surrounding the house
in absolute silence, the leaves
swarming like huge moths' wings
in a futile but tireless attempt
to come through the windows. I am so tired,
I don't understand it:
I can barely keep my eyelids open,
barely remain sitting upright.
I have been by myself
far too long watching the wind
blow through the black-green leaves.
It has been so long
since anyone has called;
I can't remember the last time
I heard the doorbell ring.
And even if it did,
what difference would it make.
I don't notice the vaguest desire
to get up and answer the door,
to see another face. No,
I could quite easily remain here
like somebody pleasantly lapsing
into deep sleep, a sleep so profound
no phone or alarm clock or doorbell
could ever reach its lightless depths.
I really have to rouse myself, maybe
even call up a friend I have missed;
or go for a walk in my neighborhood's
shady decrepitude (where do they go
when August comes, where
do they all disappear to). . .
And I fully intend to, I certainly should—
just give me a minute or two,
I am so incredibly weary
and I don't know why. I think
these leaves are wishing me
asleep.
That must be what it is.
I must have left a window open.
I can hear them all at once—

they've gotten in somehow
and now
they are covering my body. My face,
they are covering my face;
and I have passed the point
where I might have lifted my hand
to brush them away
if I'd wished to.
I am drowning, I think:
I have been drowning
now for a number of years,
and I have had the strangest dream.

ENDING

It's one of those evenings
we all know
from somewhere. It might be
the last summery day—
you feel called on to leave what you're doing
and go for a walk by yourself.
Your few vacant streets are the world.
And you might be a six-year-old child
who's finally been allowed
by his elders to enter a game
of hide-and-seek in progress.
It's getting darker fast,
and he's not supposed to be out;
but he gleefully runs off, concealing himself
with his back to a tree
that sways high overhead
among the first couple of stars.
He keeps dead still, barely breathing for pleasure,
long after they have all left.

THE MAILMAN

From the third floor window
you watch the mailman's slow progress
through the blowing snow.
As he goes from door to door

he might be searching
for a room to rent,
unsure of the address,
which he keeps stopping to check

in the outdated and now
obliterated clipping
he holds, between thickly gloved fingers,
close to his eyes

in a hunched and abruptly
simian posture
that makes you turn away,
quickly switching off the lamp.

THE BLIZZARD

You sit in the unlit room watching
a storm as it slowly erases the street
and the neighbors: on one side
the mother of four
armed and dangerous grade school aged children;
and on the other those night owls, proprietors
of an open all night drive-through drug store.
You sit in the darkening room
gazing at the vanished skyline
in the distance. How long has it been?
The room completely soundless.
The wind around the house, the ticking
snow against the windows—
for some time you've ceased to hear them
or anything else, only the silence
such constant nearby noises
finally come to. The same
way the music has passed into silence
even as you listened, yet remains
filling the air, your very presence
flickering in a last
awareness of itself . . .
You are wide awake, your eyes are even open;
yet you only notice this music
which you carefully chose for yourself
long after it's ceased. And you wonder
where you might have gone
during this absence: it seems
to be night here. Yes,
it is night in the room.
But here, too, is a lamp within reach
on a small familiar stool-like table
beside you, beside the large chair
which so closely resembles the one
in which you can still recall sitting.
You reach over to switch on this lamp and are shocked
by the telephone. You sit back and inhale
the black air deep into your lungs,
and listen to it ringing.
Then, for a while, to it not ringing.

MENTAL ILLNESS

A metaphor
one in which
the body stands
for the soul
who's busy
elsewhere
no doubt floating
face down
down
a blind reverie

POEM

The darkness—where is it?
Surrounding us
all.

If darkness is, darkness is good.

        (from a song of the Ituri
        rainforest pygmies)

THE FACE

Is there a single thing in nature
that can approach in mystery
the absolute uniqueness of any human face, first, then
its transformation from childhood to old age—

We are surrounded at every instant
by sights that ought to strike the sane
unbenumbed person tongue-tied, mute
with gratitude and terror. However,

there may be three sane people on earth
at any given time: and if
you got the chance to ask them how they do it,
they would not understand.

I think they might just stare at you
with the embarrassment of pity. Maybe smile
the way you do when children suddenly reveal a secret
preoccupation with their origins, careful not to cause them shame,

on the contrary, to evince the great congratulating pleasure
one feels in the presence of a superior talent and intelligence;
or simply as one smiles to greet a friend who's waking up,
to prove no harm awaits him, you've dealt with and banished all
                              harm.

THE LEMON GROVE

In the windless 100 degrees of eleven,
in the faintly sweet shade
of the grove just past town,
every day I would go to my tree
and sit down
with my back to it, open the notebook
and drunk with inspiration commence
describing.
It was demonstrated to me there
that nothing in the world can be described.
All attempts at self-expression
all attempts at pronouncing a place you loved
would have to be abandoned, oh
the ways the bright molested child has found to pass
                 his eerie day.
And I began to learn.
(There are hidden things waiting to utter anyone who needs
                 them.)
After days of frustration verging on blackout
some things I saw and felt there
became, in what was once their botched
depiction of a place,
a place, and the saying of it
into being the power
of loving precisely what is . . .

VAN GOGH'S "UNDERGROWTH WITH TWO FIGURES"

They are taking a walk in the woods
of early spring or waning autumn.
In van Gogh, as in the works of most great masters,
all four or five of them,
there are no symbols. (Because
there are no symbols.) Only
things as they are
things as he perceived them
during visionary states,
normal states, incandescent
and lurid hangovers, creating from nothing
breakfast for a whore's little boy, or
as usual dying of loneliness, etc.
Still, besides an older man
in a formal black but somewhat shabby
suit and a girl in what will have been
considered a long pale-green dress
from the 1960s, it is hard not to
see a skeleton with clothes on and a woman
walking two or three Eurydicean paces
right behind him (one more
slip: at least he mixed his references here).
He has on what looks like a squashed-down top hat:
Vincent the mad, most regretfully
expelled, malnourished
and no doubt tertiary syphilitic lover
of the cosmos never lost his sense of fun.
The young woman's face is dead
white, though. In fact
she has no face;
and there's nothing, incidentally,
in the least bit metaphorical about it.
I can remember seeing this, once,
outside the painting.

BOY LEAVING HOME

So it was home that left him
little by little, and not
the other way around. The others
disappearing, the house growing
emptier, gaining new rooms, one
he had so seldom entered
the view from the window
encompassed a landscape of cornfields and woods
he had never seen before—
it made his heart hurt.
Anxious trespasser, thief
who will take only what he can carry.
He thought he heard the front door open,
now he began to hear voices
filling the house, and he wondered
why he'd bothered
as long as he had
when he would not be asked to stay . . .
It would be easy enough to escape
once more—he knew all about that—
hiding under the bed until they were asleep.
He notices that he's referring to himself
as somebody else,
someone else in the past again.
But never mind that.
He is very tired of escaping;
and the reason the thought of it scares him
so much is as simple
as it always was:
absolute absence of option.
Because where?
Wherever you happen to go
it's the same thing all over again.
First, you find yourself there
waiting for you. And then
you have a place
you'll have to leave; you leave
to find a place . . .
So many rooms now, the house so much bigger,
homesickness already beginning
to tighten at his throat,
and he's not even gone. He is,
of course, quite gone. And yet
here he is—someone else figure it out.

Yes, it seems to have doubled in size;
either that or he has just turned four.
There's nothing that can't happen now.
The ceiling so high
he can lie on the bed in his sister's old room
and see the black-blue sky, as from down
in a well, stars appearing, the gold tinge of the crescent.
On some tomorrow's afternoon
all at once he will notice the light's
starting to shine through the walls.
Very faintly at first, but at last—
it is inevitable—
he will find himself staring right through them.
All the way down the untravelled
back road. And without even turning his head
on the pillow, past the crows' fields
through the first November snow,
the skeletal cornstalks gold gleam
in the woods, in what's left
of the sun.
The time has arrived to get drunk,
he's decided.
He has never done this before
and so figures he'll just mix them all:
half a glass of something dark,
then one of something transparent, in a big jar.
He fills up this jar maybe twice
and maybe more than twice,
drinking it down as if it were water—
drowning in desperate green nausea, and wondering
what it will be like when it happens.
It is harder to tell, he supposes,
when no one is there;
but he's certain that his face is altered.
Into that of someone related to him, living
a long time before he was born;
perhaps it's changed back to his old face, or forward
in time, it's the face God had prepared.
There's been some massive reconstruction
no matter how you part your hair,
but the mirrors—you cannot look in them
since each has become a starless abyss
someone is sure to fall into.
They ought to put sheets over all of them.
The telephone begins to ring:
a brief game of Russian roulette?

He has five or six seconds to decide.
Now he's going to get to hear a little music.
It seems to be a bird's voice: one
he has never heard before, or noticed.
It's producing a kind of high fugue in the octaves beyond
which nobody can hear;
he feels he could listen forever,
except he's lost the power to shut it off.
That makes a difference. You have to
watch out for these figures of speech, don't you think.
He opens his eyes all at once,
the noon sun turning everything to a white blindness.
He slowly sits up in the dead corn stubble,
all the while gazing around;
a few silent crows perched nearby
on their stalks
incuriously staring—
crows with stars for eyes.
It is snowing lightly and the moon-sized sun burns white.
It appears he is fully dressed under his coat,
someone has put his gloves on,
thoughtful. He notices he's even wearing
that ridiculous Christmas scarf
his mother knitted the year he got tall
but not tall enough to keep
from stepping on it now and then,
incurring the mirth of all.
The one he hanged himself with.
He turns his head.
The house is gone. He is relieved to note
the little Olivetti
like a miniature suitcase
placed beside him on the frozen ground.
A hangover isn't so bad—
one feels extremely courageous and lucid,
apparently.
And you need no one.
He thumbed a ride at this point, clearly.
It had been written down
for years,
it had already happened . . .
It suddenly occurs to him
that the element of grammar they call
tense, like time itself, has always been
falsely assumed to reflect some demonstrable
facet of reality—that word.

As if there was just one.
Then there's the problem of your watch,
weight, age and height
in eternity.
Let Augustine worry about it.
The glorious future awaited him,
or awaits him, the future
perfect, too. His life—
it had begun at last, and high time.
It has been over so long.

Translations

REMEMBRANCE

(Rainer Maria Rilke)

And you wait, and await the one thing
that endlessly heightens your life;
the impregnable, the unheard of,
the awakening of stone, depths
turned facing you.

The bindings bound in gold and brown
darken in their shelves;
and you think of countries
traveled through, of images,
the clothes of women lost again.

And you know all at once: it was *there*.
You rise and in front of you
stands a past year's
anguish and stature and prayer.

FROM THE NOTEBOOK FRAGMENTS OF RAINER MARIA RILKE

To drink things dissolved and diluted
with eyes used to looking through books
instead of chewing on the kernel of reality

*

From time to time the breezes move now as if bearing
invisibly the pitching of some tremendous weight.
We on the other hand have to be satisfied
with what we can see. As much as we long

to be carried out across daytime and being
into that sorrow filled with recurrence.
How can a distance be so unendingly near
yet not come any nearer—not all the way?

It was already like this once. But then
it was not a hesitating joy of early spring
set free in the wind. Perhaps the greatest things
come no closer to us—that's how the year grows,

how the soul blooms, when the season
of the soul occurs. We're none of that.
We're here because we're torn here from a great distance
and raised up and destroyed from far away.

*

Never mind one day, which pauses before the rain
and whose soundless clothing of you in itself
only a rooster crowing now and then interrupts.
Let one such day hold your face up
to the glad rosiness
of the little peach trees which like a
weeping for joy
quietly overflow.

*

No, I'm not going to be destroyed by anyone,
and I pray that I don't suddenly go blind
within, where the depths are, which endure

and hold up everything,
and I need a little fame
just enough so they may once again find me
worthy of you, and hence say of me:
This mirror was once among her possessions
and for a time belonged to her
and its silver hilt is still
surrounded by the legend of her hand
and whoever would comprehend the unending,
discover her beauty here in the brilliance
of this mirror—, which she would then present
to the solitary angel, that within it
he might catch the still too distant fires
and turn the brightening of God rising
on past darknesses and things.

*

Now we awaken with memories,
facing what was; whispered sweetness
which once pierced and spread through us
sits silently nearby with its hair all undone

*

In ignorance before the heavens of my life,
I stand amazed. Oh enormous stars.
Unfolding and descent. How still.
As though I weren't there. Do I take part in this?
Did I dispense with their pure influence? Do the tides
in my blood rise and fall in consonance with them?
I'll put away wishes, all forms of relationship,
and accustom my heart to its farthest reaches.
It does best to live among its terrifying stars,
and not in apparent protection, pacified by what's near.

*

The way water surfaces silently,
evaporate, I'm on my knees
to give you my ascending
changing face.

*

We're drawn to what is unaware of us:

to trees, which slumbrously tower beyond us,
to any Being-For-Itself, to any Keeping-Silent—
but this is really how we close the circle

which flows through all we can't possess
and back again into us, forever healing.
Oh things, to think you stand in the vicinity of the stars!
We live on, and we have done no harm

*

THE GUEST

Who *is* the guest? I was in *your* circle.
Yet every guest is something else besides his hours
                              somewhere;
for from being a guest's most primeval sources
something else takes part with him, that he
                              knows nothing of.

He comes and goes. There's nothing about him that
                              stays the same.
Yet he suddenly feels, because someone's sheltering him,
he survives in the balance of kindness
equally distant from known and unknown.

*

THE HAND

Look at the tiny bird
that has come by accident into the room:
for twenty heartbeats
it lay in a hand.
A human hand. Determined to protect.
Protective, owning nothing.
But
there on the windowsill
free
it is still deep in terror,
strange to itself
and its surroundings,
the universe—no recognition.
Ah, how confusing a hand is,
even one bent on rescue.
In the most helpful of hands

there is still death enough
and was money

*

BAUDELAIRE

The poet alone has made one the world
existing in far-scattered
fragments in each of us.
With unheard of authority
he has brought proof of beauty;
but because he himself celebrates what torments him
he has eternally consecrated defeat:

and even annihilation turns to world.

*

Regarding my answer I still don't know
when I am going to give it.
Yet, hear the rake already at work.
Above all alone in the vineyard a man's
already talking to the earth.

*

We are just mouth. Who sings the distant heart
that lives whole and complete inside all things?
Its huge pulsations are divided up in us
into small pulsations. And its huge pain
is, like its huge joy, too much for us.
So again and again we tear ourselves away
and are just mouth. But all at once
the huge heartbeat secretly breaks in on us,
so that we cry out—,
and are then being, change, and face.

*

Oh, not to be excluded,
not to be cut off
by such an insubstantial wall
from the measure of the stars.
Inner self, what is that?
If not a risen sky

through which birds are hurled, a sky
deep with the winds of return.

*

Now nothing can prevent me from
completing my appointed orbit—,
it frightens me to think a mortal could contain me.
A womb contained me once.
Breaking out of it was fatal:
I broke forth into life. But are arms so deep,
are they fertile enough, to allow for
escape from them, through the first agony
of a new birth?

*

Birds' voices are starting to praise.
And have a right to. We listen a long time.
(We're the ones in masks, oh God, and in costumes!)
What are they saying? a little insistence, a little
                              sadness, and a lot of promise
which files away at the half-divulged future.
And in-between, in our hearing, heals
the beautiful silence they break.

THE RAISING OF LAZARUS

(Rainer Maria Rilke)

Evidently, this was needed. Because people need
to be screamed at with proof.
Still, he imagined Martha and Mary
standing beside him. They would
believe he *could* do it. But no one believed,
every one of them said: Lord,
you come too late.
And he went with them to do what is not done
to nature, in its sleep.
In anger. His eyes half closed,
he asked them the way to the grave. He wept.
A few thought they noticed his tears,
and out of sheer curiosity hurried behind.
Even to walk the road there seemed monstrous
to him, an enactment, a test!
A fever erupted inside him, contempt
for their insistence on what they called
their Death—their Being Alive.
And loathing flooded his body
when he hoarsely cried: Move the stone.
By now he must stink, someone suggested
(he'd already lain there four days)—but he
stood it, erect, filled with that gesture
which rose through him, ponderously
raising his hand (a hand never lifted
itself so slowly, or more)
to its full height, shining
an instant in air . . . then clenching
in on itself, abruptly, like a claw, aghast
at the thought *all* the dead might return
from that tomb, where the enormous cocoon of
the corpse was beginning to stir.
But finally, only the one decrepit figure appeared
at the entrance—and they saw
how their vague and inaccurate
life made room for him once more.

THE ANNUNCIATION
(Rainer Maria Rilke)

It isn't just that an angel entered: realize
this is not what startled her. She might have been
somebody else, and the angel
some sunlight or, at night, the moon
occupying itself in her room—, so quietly
she accustomed herself to the form he took.
She barely suspected that this kind of visit
is exhausting to angels. (Oh if we knew
how pure she was. Didn't a deer,
catching sight of her once in the trees,
lose itself so much in looking at her
that without coupling it conceived the unicorn,
the animal of light, the pure animal!)
It's not just that he walked in, but that
he placed the face of a young man
so close to hers: his gaze and the one
with which she answered it blended
so much, suddenly, that everything else vanished
and what millions saw, built, and endured
crowded inside of her: only her and him:
seeing and seen, eye and whatever is beautiful to the eye
nowhere else but right here. *This*
is startling. And it startled them both.

Then the angel sang his song.

PIETA
(Rainer Maria Rilke)

Now my anguish is complete. It is unspeakable,
it fills me. I am numb
like the stone's core.
I am hard, and know only one thing:
you grew big—
. . . and grew big,
in order to stand outside
my heart, an agony
bigger than it is capable of.
Now you're lying right across my lap,
now I can no longer give you
birth.

QUIETING OF MARY AT THE RESURRECTION
(Rainer Maria Rilke)

What they felt at that moment: isn't it
sweeter than any other secret
and at the same time earthly:
the moment he met her, relieved, still
a little pale from the grave:
every part of him risen.
Met her first! It would be impossible
to say how much it healed them.
Yes, they were healing, that's all. Without even having to
touch each other very hard.
For hardly a second he
laid his almost
eternal hand on her woman's shoulder.
And quietly
like trees when spring comes,
endlessly at one,
they began this season
of their ultimate intimacy.

THE SICK CHILD

(Rainer Maria Rilke)

With a slight turn of the head on the pillow
his face returned to the room and observed
the state of things: they were still there.
And it occurred to him: this is all we know.

Yet even of this you could never be sure
as you lay there for days on end, staring, half conscious:
one thing took shape while another dissolved. Vagueness
rose from the mirror. But where was that

in whose presence you could always be consoled?
When, at times, even your own hand smelled
unfamiliar, and from the next room
the beloved voices sounded like company.

LES CHERCHEUSES DE POUX
(Arthur Rimbaud)

While the child's forehead, eaten with red torments,
Appeals to the white swarm of indistinct hallucinations,
Appear at his bedside two big charming sisters
With slender fingers and silver nails.

They seat the boy beside a wide open
Window, where tangled flowers float in the blue air;
Where their long and terrible fingers can walk
Seductively through his heavy damp hair.

He hears their timid breathing's chant, the viscid
Fragrance of the honey of vegetables and roses,
Now and then interrupted by a startled hiss: saliva
Or the desire for kisses sucked back from the lips.

He hears their black eyelashes flicker in the perfumed
Silences; within his drunken sleepiness
The stained nails of their sweet, electrified fingers
Crackle with the deaths of tiny lice.

Now the wine of laziness rises inside him:
A sigh into a harmonica, delirium.
He feels a longing to weep which rises and fades
Again and again to the rhythm of their caresses.

GRASS HUTS OF THE VOSGES
1939

(René Char)

Beauty, my right hand, along the hideous road,
At the milestone of courage and lamps;
I'd let myself freeze if you were December, my bride,
My future life is your face when you sleep.

FIFTEEN-YEAR-OLD BEING STRUCK
(René Char)

The identical blows which sent him flying backward transmitted him to a place, far beyond his life, where if it was necessary to bleed it would never again be for the sake of one man's evil.

Then, like a tree held erect by its roots, he came to and returned with this hidden awareness added to his youth. Finally he'd broken out, and gotten away with it; and he became entirely happy.

He made it all the way to his farthest fields, to the border of reeds whose glassy rustling he noticed for the first time. And for a while it seemed as if those,most in need of compensation and comfort might find a new parent in the least imaginary things the earth provides.

He would begin again, until this new ability to stand upright and awake among others overwhelmed the impulse, the necessity of flight, and he found himself moving beside them, superior in vulnerability.

WHISPERED CEREMONY

(René Char)

Like a kneeling communicant offering his candle
The white scorpion has lifted its lance and touched
                                        the right spot.
Ambush has instructed it in invisible agility.
Swollen currents will ravage this naive scene.
Narcissus, gold buttons undoing themselves in the
                                        field's heart.
The king of the alders is dying.

LINE OF FAITH
(René Char)

The grace of the stars resides in their compelling us to speak, in show-
ing us we are not all alone, that the dawn has a ceiling and my fire your
two hands.

RECEIVING ORION
(René Char)

Who are you looking for dark bees
Among the awakening lavender?
Your slave the king
Is passing.
Blind,
He sows;
A hunter, he flees
The flowers that follow him.
He bends his bow and every creature shines!
His night is tall; think it over, arrows.

The earth is honey to a mortal meteor.

POEM
(Ingeborg Bachmann)

In the valley that's plowed
through this speechlessness
a single word, attracting
vast forests to the site, until
my mouth lies
completely in shade.

THE SINGER
(Guillaume Apollinaire)

And the one-string trumpets of the sea

New Poems

FOUR O'CLOCK

Wind from the stars—
everything will be forgotten.
The solitary bird's voice.
I wake and close my eyes.

CHILD REARING

He stood in the doorway
absently gazing
into the room: she had left
the doll with its head on
the pillow, the sheet
drawn neatly up over its face.
At last he went to work.
The morning light stood in the doorway.

ENCOUNTER 3 A.M.

She stepped out of a doorway on 86th Street
startling me badly, and softly spoke
a word that might have been my name—
a pretty fourteen-year-old maybe, in black denim

jacket and skirt not designed with your midwinter
night wind chill factor in mind;
one who somewhat resembled a very tall child
who'd botched her first secret attempt

at trying on her mother's make-up.
I felt nothing now but a dismal desire
to talk, maybe offer to take her
someplace to purchase a coat like an idiot.

But finally I did
what lots of normal men would do,
given the chance.
I started walking, fast, and turned my back on her.

THE SHORE

for Donna Edelbaum

At dawn a silence breaks. First
light and the surf still sounds faintly
like a woman who has lain awake
methodically tearing her sheets
into strips all night long.
She is finally drifting off now.
On her back, hair and skin damp
with the salt of her body she notices
the smell, a faraway perfume
combined with blood just like the ocean's;
she gazes down the length of her,
black hair's long soaked strands curled
there on the dead white circles of
breasts half submerged, only breaking the water,
white belly shimmering greenly
phosphorescent: below
the tiny curls she runs her fingers through,
letting the hand float away like a sigh
which follows her soft cry—
some hidden bird she knows nothing about.
Finally she can ease her head back
on water, close her eyes and let it suck her
toward the opening sea, as she leaves
the awakening world.

FROM A ROADSIDE MOTEL

I dial but am told
I have reached the wrong party.
I make two unsuccessful
attempts after that.

My call is finally answered
by the identical stranger
who confides,
in a murderous whisper,

that no one by your name
has ever lived
at her number, familiar to me
as my own.

I sit on the edge
of the bed,
holding a phone
to my head.

NIGHT BROWSING

Lights coming on in windows
windows lit all night long

suddenly dark—. . .
He seems to sleep, head nested

in his crossed arms
on the desk, as he listens

to the first raindrops
striking the window,

the faint roar of aircraft
just vanishing

on the horizon, the phrase
underlined by himself.

AFTER CELAN

Once
when death had no vacancy,
you came and stayed in me.

AUTOBIOGRAPHY

One eventual ghost,
one in a long line

extending back
to an unthinkable origin,

just like anyone
I've ever met, or cared for, ever

laid eyes on, been glanced at
or spoken to by,

touched by,
been struck by

or struck—or with endless longing and tenderness

touched, forgot the name
and never saw again.

Reverie of the Life Cast

So take my arm and guide me
through traffic to the library.
And look up my name, if it's listed,
in that heavy book of the forgotten

with their tiny bibliographies.
And read me my last known address.
I remember so clearly the sky.
Like fear on an unconscious face.

I could ask for some shoes,
my old coat. And who knows—
they might still have the typewriter stored there.

They no longer make ribbons for those?

Yes, naturally I can see that!
Tactful of you by the way. You know: date of demise?

And you're right. Another time, another time.

FIRST DAY ON THE WARD

A blizzard. I can't see
a single person on the street.
I know they're out there, though: the fittest
reading the paper and drinking their coffee,
winter light filling the rooms where they sit
unaghast.

It's Monday in the world,
and time to go—

I've unpacked and have nothing to do
but lie down and stare at the snow.
Which is something I am good at;
something I enjoy.
Probably I'll die like this,
a long time ago.

SUNDAY AFTERNOON

My brother is deep in his library book. Which is causing my stepfather great agitation: he keeps appearing in the doorway and staring at the back of his head.

What he'd like to do is drag him downstairs to the basement for a tablesaw lesson.

He'd like to take him for a fear ride to the barber.

In the crib, left alone to her own weird devices, my sister is spending her nap time engaged in a babbling rehearsal of several recently acquired terms of abuse and grotesquely penitential self-loathing. And I,

I'm in the kitchen busy getting in my mother's way.

At the moment she's basting something that looks like a brain.

The rain continues falling. But then, it's always falling. It is Sunday, somewhere

a bell keeps on tolling.

Somebody must have been born.

METAPHOR

Then the point comes
when language decides
to start strangling itself
on its leash, make a break for it
or to turn on you—
no longer the mournful
appearing, intelligent
and silent being who guided you
in a dark world.

A Body Describes Itself

I was desolate
like a poor person's shoe.
One worn by somebody
with a bad limp,

with one foot
in the grave,
you might say:
destinationless,

blindered
by humiliation,
or in a rage
of transparently feigned occupation;

or just taking a rest,
a brief nap in an alley,
the rats hurdling his leg—
stretched out on his personal bench in the park . . .

an ugly, a disgusting shoe
abruptly uninhabited.

HAVE YOU SEEN THIS CHILD

Eating breakfast you notice
your face on the milk carton
And how old you feel

for twelve

And how will anybody ever recognize you
now but clearly
the search was called off
long ago

Nobody's looking for you
anymore nobody cares

No one is expecting you

where other people are living
kindly
people who're younger
than you with a boy
of their own

Yes

He looks a little like you

He and his mother still share the same name though

While nobody knows yours
they don't even hear

when you knock
and the young mother opens the door looks

up and down the street with
worried glances
which take in all the stars before

she closes the door
You hear the lock click

and watch as she wanders from room
to room the lights go
one by
one out

out

THE WOUND
for Denis Johnson

The very grave wound which receives proper treatment does nicely over time. As a rule it is almost instantly responsive to attention, displaying minimal resistance to medications and gradually resuming a productive, socially active and generally well-adjusted life. Interestingly, a number of more or less identical traumas never seek treatment at all and yet, once again with the passage of time, enjoy a total recovery. And for reasons not well understood a fair percentage of much less deplorable injuries fail to react to the most radical procedures: these minor gashes may remain an endless source of irritation, not to mention financial anxiety, both to their families and society at large, and simply refuse to cooperate. They are certainly going to require close monitoring; they need to be routinely probed, and great improvement is far from inevitable—on the contrary. Too often they deteriorate into chronic complainers and obscurantists. In an unprecedented instance, one actually requested permission to recite a short poem. However, our fifty minutes were up, I quickly retaped it, and the subject never arose again.

PATIENT INTERACTION

Time for one more?
Come on in,
the nicatorium's all yours.

Mind if I stare?

Don't worry:
haven't said a word
all day, and don't intend to
now.

Consider yourself
all alone.

Vesperal rain at the window.

FAILING

It's pulling me under
like heavy sedation
someone in white came
administering,
someone all in light now
for a very long instant, then
dark, all in dark
just like me

before someone arrived
to be me.
And much later,

but all by himself this time, found
in lightlessness the other door
which opened for him alone—
opened at words,
words that turned black
into sound, into both

a place represented, supposedly,
and pure noises
of breath in the world;
an unheard

of music in the reader's eyes, the soundless
music of what's yet to be,
of what can be seen but won't be . . .

I would like to be more clear.
It is so clear to me.
So I am twice alone.

But I am living twice,
as well.
I am in two places, the music
and meaning.
                Then
all at once

                I don't know, I forget—
disappointment or exhaustion

pulls me under
like heavy sedation.

And it is a relief.
What I wanted: it is too hard.

Yes I am starting to like this
much better, the
not having to be
in one place or the other.
The world

I attempted to utter, I leave that
to others not born
to their own moments yet

and let my eyes close:
one mouth pronouncing
as one with the gone
billions the radiant noun
surrounding the unending
dark

that comes before we live—

GETTING OFF WORK

I'm finished. It's finished
with me.

There is nothing to do now,
at last,

but get from this chair
to the bed

before the green prelight, the leaves'
last night telling's

obliterated by another
morning's thermonuclear

soundless detonation —
nothing

except to be quiet
enough not to wake you.

To be quiet enough
not to wake.

TO MYSELF

You are riding the bus again
burrowing into the blackness of Interstate 80,
the sole passenger

with an overhead light on.
And I am with you.
I'm the interminable fields you can't see,

the little lights off in the distance
(in one of those rooms we are
living) and I am the rain

and the others all
around you, and the loneliness you love,
and the universe that loves you specifically, maybe,

and the catastrophic dawn,
the nicotine crawling on your skin—
and when you begin

to cough I won't cover my face,
and if you vomit this time I will hold you:
everything's going to be fine

I will whisper.
It won't always be like this.
I am going to buy you a sandwich.

UNTITLED

If I think *I* have problems
I look in the mirror;
I go to the window, or
ponder the future reduced
to more or less
three pounds of haunted meat.
And it's never
like I always said:
if you don't want something
wish for it . . .
Lost in the beautiful world
I can no longer perceive
but only, now and then,
imagine
or recall—
First the long sinister youth
and then the dying man
who talks to old friends
teachers, doctors
but they don't understand
the way we feel.

FIRST LIGHT

It's raining
in a dead language.

The empty house filled with the sound

of your name
abruptly whispered,

once,

before you finally slept.

ACKNOWLEDGMENTS

Many of these poems (or primitive versions of them) first appeared in the following periodicals: *Agni Review, Blades, Columbia Magazine, Crazyhorse, Durak, Field, Ironwood, Kayak, Lynx, Missouri Review, New Honolulu Review, The New Yorker, Paris Review, Ploughshares, Provincetown Arts, Quarry West, Quarterly West, Raccoon, Shankpainter, Seneca Review, Skyline, TriQuarterly, Virginia Quarterly Review.*

Some of these poems have appeared in the following anthologies: *Best American Poetry: 1992* (Scribner's), *A Book of Luminous Things* (Harcourt Brace), *Cape Discovery* (Sheep Meadow), *The Longman Anthology of Contemporary American Poetry* and *New American Poets of the '90s* (Godine).

For permission to reprint most of these selections, the author wishes to thank the editors of the following presses: Carnegie-Mellon University, Cleveland State University, Deep Forest, Lost Roads, Minatoby, Pym-Randall, Short Line Editions and Triskelion.

For their generous assistance over the years, the author also wishes to thank the National Endowment for the Arts, the Guggenheim Foundation and the Whiting Foundation.

For helping him complete this book and for their lasting friendship, he is inexpressibly grateful to Stuart Friebert, Donald Justice, Thomas Lux, Martha McCollough, Elizabeth Oehlkers, Jordy Powers, Charles Simic and David Young.

ABOUT THE AUTHOR

Since assembling *Ill Lit* in 1998, Franz Wright has published three further collections: *The Beforelife, Walking to Martha's Vineyard,* and *God's Silence.* The first of these was a finalist for the 2001 Pulitzer Prize and the second received the 2003 Pulitzer Prize. The recipient of many other awards and fellowships, Wright now lives in Waltham, Massachusetts, with his wife, the translator and writer Elizabeth Oehlkers Wright.

COLOPHON

Designed by Steve Farkas.
Composed by Professional Book Compositors using Galliard 9½ point text type and Impact display type. Printed and bound by Edwards Brothers using 55# EB natural offset acid-free paper.